a curious beatitude

a curious beatitude

sarah klassen

The Muses' Company Series Editor: Catherine Hunter
Book design by Terry Gallagher/Doowah Design Inc.
Cover photograph by Joan Baker
Author photo by Patty Boge
Printed and bound in Canada

We acknowledge the financial support of the Manitoba Arts Council, The Canada Council for the Arts and the Government of Canada through the Book Publishing Industry Development Program (BPIDP) for our publishing program.

Library and Archives Canada Cataloguing in Publication

Klassen, Sarah, 1932-
        A curious beatitude/Sarah Klassen.

Poems.
ISBN 1-897289-04-9

I. Title.
PS8571.L386C87 2006   C811'.54   C2006-900900-7

J. Gordon Shillingford Publishing
P.O. Box 86, RPO Corydon Avenue, Winnipeg, MB Canada R3M 3S3

Contents

Requiem and *Magnificat*

This World is not Conclusion.
A Species stands beyond—
Invisible, as Music—
But—positive, as Sound—
                    —Emily Dickinson

A Curious Beatitude
(Upon hearing Brahms's *Ein Deutsches Requiem*)

1. *Selig sind die da Leid tragen*
    (Blest are those who carry sorrow)

[handwritten: Blessed are …]

Now everything is ready. Lights in the concert hall
dim down. Up on stage, the maestro
cues chorus and orchestra. An overture—
and the *requiem* begins.

> Congolese women lithe as saplings
> balance firewood, baskets of mangoes,
> manioc soaked in the river
> and sorrow on their heads.

> No one knows what grief the woman down the street
> conceals, lugging laundry to the laundromat,
> groceries in clumsy bags to the parked van,
> her cranky child from the garage to house to bed.

> And Eve. She must have carried sorrow like a stone.
> Her firstborn murdered, second son a murderer,
> the seductive apple tree, the garden
> gone for good.

Voices and violins carry the melody
with gravity. It floats up to the loges,
balconies lean in. There's an almost-gasp,
a bursting in the ear, a curious

unstopping. In the darkened hall,
lightness, as if a load is jettisoned.
As if an albatross-
burden slides into the sea.

2. *Denn alles Fleisch es ist wie Grass*
   (For all flesh is as grass)

Lately I am weight-lifting to curb upper arm flab.
Call it penitence. Call it atonement
for transgression and omission. I am listening
to the CBC's long litany: surfeit of sweetness,
meals cooked up too swiftly.
Our children burdened with obesity.

Hamlet proclaimed flesh *too, too solid.*
Wanted it melted.
A melancholic strain had long hummed in his veins.
He's been pale for centuries and thin, though wiry.
When his body's blood is poisoned, spilt,
before the arm that dropped the rapier stiffens,
before *flights of angels* catch the conductor's cue,

he'll rise, unsteady, on one elbow from his death,
speak with a princely voice, not of time's brevity
but its continuance.
                          The hall is hushed
in expectation of a reverent entry,
free of weight, into a rest so absolute, so still
you hear breath rise, a vapour from the prairie's lung.
Buffalo grass, foxtail, thin blades of bluestem
singing.

3. *Herr, lehre doch mich*
    Das ein Ende mit mir haben muss
    (Lord, teach me that my end must come)

A child aces addition and subtraction,
masters multiplication, even long division,
may one day sail through geometry, adore algebra,
trip over trigonometry,
and despite titillating correlation
between music and mathematics,
decline calculus.

A lovely, random ray of light erases
calculations on a flip chart.
Obliterates the glitches on a page.

End of day:
What has the homework-toting, dawdling child
left to get by heart? What lesson
waits in the suburban street, the lane, the concrete
driveway leading home?

(Will the child thrive? Will languages,
philosophy, material sciences, the law
stake claims? Awaken curiosity?
Will he or she love rock, jazz, classical music?
Appreciate the cadence of a *requiem?*)

The child, half-grown, slows down
for cracks in the asphalt,
hesitates at empty corners,
stalls beside an overflowing trash can,
the squashed body of a swallow unaccountably fallen

                        and stops
as if to calculate. As if
to let an unpredicted
probability
sink in.

4. *Wie lieblich sind deine Wohnungen*
    (How lovely are your dwellings)

Almost overnight, an excavation. Walls roughed up,
roof pitched on the vacant property.
Structure displacing emptiness. Construction
crews where casual cats and the wind roamed.

No one's children played there.
No one restrained the dandelions.
Fences sag as if their joints are worn.
Paint peels like dessicated skin.

Your aging father after supper begs:
take me home. He knows wherever home is,
it's not here. Not this third floor cell,
this loneliness, this meagre light.

Where shall we house the weariness?
What dwelling's cosy and commodious,
illuminated but not blinding, workmanship
still under warranty, air uniformly wholesome?

To complete the picture you will need trees
planted near a lucent stream, fruit ripening,
birds light as dandelion down seeking respite
from the never-setting sun. And carolling.

5. *Ihr habt nun Traurigkeit*
   (You have sorrow now)

This is by far *The Saddest Music in the World*.
You want it sung when hope is laid to rest
like the fallen vireo a gardener finds and cradles
in earth. You want it for the children
hunkered near graves of mothers
and fathers dead of AIDS in Africa.

You want this music for your swan song
when you leave unwillingly
the stage where you have flickered
briefly, rarely
shone, and sometimes strutted stupidly.

When you are far from home you want
its gloomy harmonies, its downcast beauty.

> The first notes came to Brahms
> when death had put an end to Robert
> Schumann's music. A companionship.
> Brahms wrung from that bereavement
> cadences. When his beloved mother died
> the music kept on coming. Out of grief
> he made a *Requiem*, in German.
> Out of sorrow, solace.

Neither the treble voices of The Anonymous Four
lamenting unaccompanied the plight of wayfaring
strangers yearning for a sweet hereafter,
nor the minor melodies an orthodox male choir sings
evenings, *a capella*, during Lent,
nor blues nor jazz can offer this much
sadness. It leaves you curiously
undone. It leaves you
comforted.

6. *Denn wir haben hie keine bleibende Stadt*
   (We have no permanent city here)

Baghdad bombed. New York assaulted
on a flawless, teal-blue morning,
Jerusalem built on rubble of the blest
city once named Salem.

Invisible cities Calvino conjured shimmer
behind closed eyes. Ancient Atlantis,
somnolent under water, waits
for a not-yet-born Ulysses to locate it.

> Woodwinds and grieving strings
> accompany the yearning of soprano, alto
> tenor and baritone, for the city of peace,
> unmarred, illuminated, permanent.

Will TV kids, afflicted with
unsightly wounds earth-dwellers carry,
believe hope is not lost, not all
have lost it? In New York

architects draft blueprints of a future
habitation in the emptiness. In Baghdad
looters scrabbling through rubble
excavate from under time and twisted steel:

antiquities. Their worth soars way beyond
words. Try saying them. Say: *Tigris*
and *Euphrates*. Say: *Eden*. Say: *garden*.
The tree of life. The golden apple.

Slowly, with what's left of breath, say
Salem.

7. *Selig sind die Toten*
   (Blest are the dead)

A blessing before those most needing it leave.
The anthem fades. The last clump of earth
thuds on the coffin lid. The undertaker offers
the bereaved blood-red carnations
shrouded in a brace of baby's breath.

Mourners rally around last words,
last wishes. They must negotiate life
insurance, unpaid debts,
testaments, unlisted
objects waiting for possession.

Those left behind could use a blessing.
Memory of derailed or broken off
conversations erased. Rift and rending
assuaged. A retroactive
reconciliation.

But this beatitude's intended for the dead
as though, although departed, they remain
with us. As if sorrow becomes blessing;
poverty an asset; loss, gain. As if
the earth that covers them still
waits to be inherited.

n *Sanctus*: program notes

In Cairo
the composer with his tape recorder
hears the call to prayer:
> *God is great.*

The metropolis lit up like a stadium,
the heavens riven with glory.

At night in Gulu
he records a rain song. Latigo Oteng sings it
while his fingers pluck accompaniment
from the seven-stringed Enango.
Rain falls on Uganda. A tentative plop, plop
then drumming, then
the menacing deluge.
> *He was crucified for us*
> *Buried*
> *And on the third day*
> *Rose again.*

At Lake Kyogo the composer
listens to lamentation
poured on the stiffening body
of the drowned fisherman.
A stifling papyrus hut
the scent of death
mother and wife wailing:
> *Our Father who art in heaven*
> *May your hallowed will be done.*

The composer (a foreigner in Africa)
discovers the cattle song, the Masai
milking song, the lovely river song
and war drums thrumming in the distance.

In Sudan he rides a camel in the desert
beneath a reticent moon, alone.
Tribesmen on remote mountains recite the Koran.
The cooling sand is singing.

Holy, holy, holy
Lord God of hosts
Maker of heaven and earth
And all things visible
And invisible.

A shepherd boy plucks the harp he made
of wire and wood. Melodic breath. A prayer.
An *Agnus Dei*.

His mother, stepping from the tent,
strikes a bell proclaiming the birth
of a boy. A brother. Another
hungry lamb of God.
      Gloria.

After the courtship dance, the women's
bravery dance, the trumpet dance
the foreigner comes home believing
      God
      Whose glory fills the heavens
      Will have mercy
      On Uganda, Kenya, Cairo
      And Sudan
      Christ
      will have mercy

on refugees unsure which song to sing
accompanied by homemade drum
or thumb piano, the Zande family
fleeing bloodshed, praising their deliverer
and the devout traveller who heard
frogs croaking in a swamp in Africa.

He will make of everything a *Credo*
(with piano solo)
fervent *Kyrie* (for choir).
He wants to sing (with every vibrant cord
and pipe and ligament) for Africa,
a *Sanctus.* For all the world,
a song.

17

Magnificat

Hodie Christus natus est

She has no shoulders. You've noticed this
before the exultation of the Byzantine
Alleluia. She has arms:
the sleeves of her shirt aren't empty.
She folds them tight, as if
they are wayward wings,
or she finds the rotunda cold.
Vocal overtones float upward to the dome
on air, on radiant vowels, on violins.
Behold the classic profile of her face
when she turns
during Andrew Balfour's tender *Ave
Maria.* She has ivory skin
like the soprano soloist. A lovely mouth.
A brass ensemble joins the voices: Giovanni
Gabrieli's magnificent
Magnificat. At the applause
you catch her clapping. Look at her fingers.
Four slender digits, one apparently prehensile,
much too long for a thumb. Can't hope to lift
an instrument with that half-hand
raised unselfconsciously to touch her golden hair.
        (Is it thalidomide, flawed genes, advanced
        arthritis?)
Violas raise Bach's jubilant *Et Incarnatus Est*
and the concert's over.
The woman with no shoulders, you,
the enthralled, imperfect listeners, released,
descend the marble stairs and spill
just as they are
into the dissonant wind, the muscled
arms of winter.

Intermission

Adroit lighting and a stylish set.
The tenor prepared to gamble almost
everything, though not for love. The sweet
soprano will not live; she is too innocent.
Nor the old woman with her rage.
Violins crescendo, fade.

At half-time promenade, a glint of diamonds,
laughter, the indiscreet
swirl and swish of spilled secrets.

White-aproned women at the bar
spill nothing when they pour thick chocolate
hot from a thermos into a porcelain demitasse.
You dip a silver spoon in
sweetness. The midnight velvet

curtain rises for the last act. The pretty soprano
drowns like Ophelia in a well of darkness.
The old woman's ghost, enraged,
flashes three fatal cards.

Another spill of blood.

The tenor drinks and bids
the ace against the Queen of Spades. Finale
without sweetness. Darkness
without intermission.

What the Boat Carries

On the churning sea a small blue boat.
Wind smooths the yellow sail and pins it flat
against the fitful sky. Sky over Galilee
was agitated, water olive-
green, white-capped and snarling.

Two shrouded figures in the stern. Women?
Which one's the sailor, which one prophesies
rough passage? Four able hands lie idle.
The travellers look ahead, steadfast, as if
they've seen Christ walking on the waves.

Who are they?
Why did they embark?
What voice or circumstance persuaded them
to climb in-
to the empty hold?

They've brought no luggage for the voyage.
No munchies, no bottle of water.
No oars and no one asleep in the hold.
There's no visible tiller. Not one life preserver.
What absent captain guides this boat,

the yellow sail so radiant it blinds?
Pigment laid on with zeal. The artist's
vision of arrival at safe harbour,
desire to awaken sleepers,
to catch before storm breaks

above the hollow boat a blazing
portion of the sun.

Mystical Boat
Odilon Redon, Pastel and black chalk on buff-coloured wove paper

The Weight of Opulence

Hundreds of bunched blossoms meant for market.
An extravagance. Even the canvas bands binding the cargo
to the man's back and broad shoulders shine like gold.
The man himself on all fours (beast of burden
or the Christ collapsed bearing the cross)
bright as the noonday sun.

The woman's hands balance the overfilled basket
weighing the man down.
She steadies the radiant load, her body *clothed*
with the sun, warm and fruitful.
Her eyes, neither starry nor banal, follow the labourer
who rises, carries the beauty away from her side,

out of sight. She is left
alone in the garden, pruning, weeding.
Around her a buzz of bees, the cloying fragrance,
weight of heat. She will steel her heart
to hear his cry, his plaintive: Come,
come and buy.

The Flower Carrier
Diego Rivera, 1935, Oil and tempera on masonite

On the Road

Are we almost there? the kids ask. Their mother
daydreams a Dairy Queen enthroned in a prairie town
before hunger overtakes them. They've run out
of bottled water. Patience. The long-suffering
driver-Dad, in need of caffeine, lurches toward sleep.
Reduce speed, his wife commands. Turn circum-
spectly off the highway, stop for a quick nap.

The road's relentless. The summer evening won't wind down.
Sun beams its low, slow rays, painting the clouds'
unguarded underside. The travelling family
illuminated. An exhausted father in a rust-brown cloak
sprawls like an awkward interlude across a gunny sack,
eyes shut. The saintly beard points up. The sack?
The refugee family's worldly goods. Food for the journey.

The naked baby at his homeless mother's breast
does not inquire, feeding, how far, or when
he will enter the temple, astound scholars, baffle the devil
in Judea's desert, tend troublesome sheep. Still many storms,
still many star-lit nights at his mother's heart
before he learns to measure wood, hammer the nails home,
shoulder timber and transgression. Suffering

a mother's dread, Mary will cajole and scold, Be careful.
The stolid, earth-brown donkey standing sentinel
waits for morning. For the long slogging haul.
When Dad wakes, groggy, Mom will say,
Let's hit the road before the kids rouse,
ravenous. She hasn't slept one wink. Hasn't dared
dream her children grown, barrelling headlong

along a pot-holed road. The eye will search
for certain destination, a reliable conveyance
on that untried way. Where do the travel-weary eat
and shelter? When will the sun go down?
The gusty prairie wind let up?
How, and in what country, does the journey end?

The Rest on the Flight into Egypt
Orazio Gentileschi, c.1620, Oil on canvas

Abstract with Mermaids

Right off the bat you believe: finger painting.
A sassy child smacked chubby hands in the paint pot
and undetained by boundaries, unfettered by instruction,
covered a canvas with squiggles and swirls.
Not something you can lightly hang experience on,

though the green streaks resemble branches,
that yellow blob the sun, and this rough orange
splotch interrupting a patch of indigo
is the frisbee moon viewed from a certain angle.
A distorted football, if you like, or

the horrible, severed head of John the Baptist.
The stained platter, perhaps, on which
it was delivered to Salome. So much to answer for.
So much for abstraction. Below the indigo,
thick brick and ochre brush strokes

invoke a school of mermaids intertwined
with undulant seaweed. The sheer notion
of joy or buoyant fantasy. An urge to overleap
boundaries between this and that other world.
On either side of the sportive mermaids

two elements float free, detached
from the rest of the picture. To the right
a vertical scarlet streak and to the left
an ink-black spiral. The streak is blood
set savagely in motion. The spiral,

the dark wheel of fate. No innocent
girl or boy had a hand in this
darkness. A heavy step, hard-breathing
malice skews the choreography. The painting
blotched. The play of mermaids, marred.

A Vision of the Mermaids
Mali Morris, 1983, Acrylic on canvas

Fiction

The room is occupied, the queen-sized bed
made up, immaculate. So ordinary,
chocolates and a pink rose on the pillow
would be absurd.

Closed luggage in a corner on the floor.
A ridiculous hat struts on the shelf and a floral
dress lies draped, defeated on the green chair.
Fiction lurks in the freshly painted corners.

Like sleuths pursuing source and efficacy
of light, we scan the hotel room walls:
a large pale panel and the smaller square, opaque,
egg-yellow. Egg shell draperies pass muster.

And now we can no longer disregard
the woman sitting on the bed, half-nude,
her brooding face, her still-young body shadowed,
a folded letter in her birdlike hands.

It's not her semi-nakedness alone disturbs
nor ink-black shadows under the bed.
Not knowing which bright panel is the window
troubles us.

Not knowing the letter's intent. The sender.
A single sentence could condemn the woman:
she'd be obliged to throw her dress on, don the hat,
grab the unopened bags. She'd thrust her feet into

the kicked-off, high-heeled shoes we overlooked,
and leaving no excuses for the viewer, no note, no tip
at the front desk, check out of the newly-painted room.
The meticulous hotel.

Hotel Room
Edward Hopper, 1931, Oil on canvas

Landscape with Rainbow

Anyone with a box of crayons could draw
that vivid rainbow: a memorized spectrum,
a merging of tone and hue.

The granary's too plain.
A school girl would add windows and a door,
chimney with smoke rising

like a sweet beatitude. There should be laughter,
children tumbling in the wind-blown grass. A path.
A verdant garden. A woman

waiting in the open door. A farm boy
would crayon a red tractor in the furrowed field, a cultivator,
fertilizer spreader, harvester with an air-conditioned cab.

The rain is over.
The treeless landscape though unpeopled
is inhabited: one bright foot of the rainbow

anchored in brown earth, the other
striding off the picture's edge. The fearless arc
bisects the sea-blue sky:

one half of heaven for the girl,
the farm boy gets the rest. For both of them:
the seeded field basking in light,

the weathered granary, the mud
road winding past the seven
colours of the rainbow.

Study For She Did Not Turn
David Inshaw, 1974, Oil on canvas

Love

The artist adored these four pears,
wanted with all her heart to preserve them
from shrivelling, bruising, losing their juicy taste,
their sumptuous colour. Wanted them round
and lucent. The first two lean into each other
for companionship or even love. The third
sits upright behind the second which overlaps it
only slightly. In the seductive gap that opens
between the third pear and the fourth,
both light and shadow shimmer. In that dimension
a silent presence holds in charge
the beauty of the fruit.
                                    Stillness mitigates
the fourth pear's solitary opulence,
its fervent glow,
its well-nigh hopeless yearning.

Four Pears No.3
Martha Alf, 1986, Coloured pencil on paper

Landscape with Angel

An angel, wings streaming like a declaration,
occupies one-half the sky. Her solid body
hangs above the docile field. Sheep, shed,
haystack and hedges decorate a muted landscape
as if an artisan with yarn and needle stitched them.
Contours of hills and trees, their tints, their homely
textures inscribe the countryside.
Easy to overlook small pools of blue
water the livestock seek at evening.

The angel of course moves nowhere
of her own accord. She merely hovers, knowing
an angel's place should remain modest.
A constant witness to forever-turning seasons,
curiously-hued heavens, the charming picture's
implied expectation: sheep-shearing and harvest.
An angel worth her salt will record simply.
(Evenings, the jostling herd's raw thirst
is quenched at quiet pools of water.)

Angel in the Sky
Margaret Neve, 1987, Oil on wood panel

Woman in a Blue Dress

And you, what are you staring at? What
winter narrative, tableau, enticing still life
beyond the frosted window draws your gaze,
demands unwavering attention night and day?

You overlook the cluttered room I work in:
messy table top, computer, printer running,
lament of a superannuated fridge obliterating
with its wintry one-note drone all silence.

Can you hear?

The world glints with the spark of steel.
My neighbour's children play on the hard white
mountain the plow shoved up, their cold cheeks,
fiery coals. Their laughter, broken glass.

Contained in a sombre frame, you are
constrained to face the east. Do you mind?
Holgate has painted you a midnight dress,
first light playing in the sheer

folds of sleeves. Clasped hands idle,
you are silent. Intelligent. Your eyes open
to the choreography of scarf-and-parka people,
maples weighted down with snow.

Are you waiting for the mellow days of summer?
Garbage pick up? Mail delivery? Long-delayed
change of scene?
The future?

Listen.

I'll write you into narrative.
You'll be the tragic character, the ingénue
who leaves home, trades a familiar landscape
for alien ground, true love for a seducer

destined to be untrue. You'll be the delectable
woman predators believe they recognize.
They do not know as Holgate knows
(and I begin to know) that no one can

be certain what you are. Keep mind and spirit
steady, my girl, your dark eyes open.
When all the chips are down, remember
the advice your mother gave you

and you spurned, as any adolescent would.
Be quick to catch the providential
strokes of fortune when (and
if) they come your way.

Don't be afraid. I promise you *this*
portion of my wall will be reserved
for you. For now.
About the unveiled years remaining

let me say (as if I were your mother)
I will love you through the season's
alterations. The tabletop may never be
uncluttered. You will hear the furnace fan,

the fridge forever humming.
Neither you nor I can stop the sun
rising like a benediction in the east
and blinding us.

Ludovine
Edwin H. Holgate, c.1930

Vacation on Saturna Island

1.
This is a moonscape and a girl in blue
flowered dress flies across the pocks and crevices,
hair streaming like the outpoured morning sun.
She's got a smooth grey stone cradled in one hand,
a sturdy stick gripped in the other.
Her light feet, winged and sandaled,
barely touch the rough terrain.
Her child face shines.

Where is she going now? her mother asks
as the camera clicks and captures
the girl in headlong flight she fears
might fling her out of the picture.
She wishes the stone in her daughter's hand
were white and had a name engraved,
the stick not quite so fiercely pointed
at both ends. She wishes she
had means to make a rough path plain.

2.
Toward evening someone hollers:
Orca whales are headed for the island.
Mother and daughter run to the rocky edge
of the moon and hold breath in
until they see the water troubled by the vision
they've been waiting for: three massive heads,
three dorsal fins move closer
without haste or hesitation. Silent and grand
they come. They swim the island's length
and vanish into distance.

The daughter reaches with her hand as if
she wants to follow the receding creatures
to where they sleep.
The mother's glad the girl has seen what she has seen.
The sun is low and will be lower.
The water, troubled, ripples at the crater's edge.
Above them: a flat white stone, cold, ghostly
in a midnight ocean. When morning comes,
the mother warns her girl, you'll see
an empty sky. An empty ocean.

Photos by Joan Baker

The Far Country

Bravely in a land of dust
we set out, as pilgrims must,
you, who fear the dark, and I
fearing winter in the sky.
                    —Denise Levertov

The wind blows where it chooses—
                    —John 3: 9 NRSV

Three Questions

Where do we come from? Paul Gauguin
sojourning in a foreign country,
heart-broken, asked. As if he didn't know
the various versions. How we were made
from ash and mud, called out of water,
summoned from the sky, an unexpected wind
blowing breath into us. Who hasn't heard
of Glooscap, Gilgamesh. The turtle. Frog.
And Michelangelo in Rome painting in oil
and agony the volatile finger of God.

What are we? Now
that's a different story,
embracing more than flailing limbs,
the out thrust chest, visage
the steamed-up mirror offers us
at daybreak. We want to know:
was there a plan behind all this?
Was thought given (how much,
how competent)? What else (or who)
has been invested in the enterprise?

Where are we going?
Wouldn't we all just love to know
the climate of that country,
its prevailing winds, the seasons'
wistful turning, patterns of
precipitation, socio-
economic structures.
Politics. Tell us the twists,
the hairpin turns of the road,
time that must elapse before arrival.
Places of rest along the way.
The destination.

Gauguin, grieving
the death of his favourite daughter,
sits in the shade of a shanty
in Tahiti. Bougainvillea bushes bloom
and pink hibiscus. The sky is ocean blue,
the women's dresses in luxuriant
landscapes glow like the primary colours
in a painter's palette. His favourite
brushes are idle. The stretched-out canvas
empty as the pretty clouds that drift
languidly across the sky.

Postcards from the Andes

1.City of gold

Pizarro, chasing down the sun, found himself
in the world's navel: Cusco, golden city of his dreams.
He'd promised his men if they conquered
dreams of home, survived the ocean and the Andes,
they could count on gold stacked like wood or lumps of coal.
A stake in Eldorado worth dying for.

Atahuallpa, Inca king, son of the sun,
had never learned to read, would never die.
He died. A small finch sang. The patient vultures
drew crude circles in the sky.

When the last stone storehouse was emptied
of the last gold nugget, the Spaniards tore down Cusco,
temples, everything. A few foundations remained.
Magnificent cathedrals Europeans fashioned collapsed
when the affronted earth beneath the Andes quaked.

Unless they were built on stones laid by architects
and builders who had never seen a blueprint,
could not read instructions and until the day they died
staked everything on the unfailing
wisdom of the sun.

2. Precipice

Our Macchu Piccu guide gathers us like llamas
on the rough trail. He stands astride,
facing his flock, bronzed Inca warrior,
ebony eyes scanning the Andes.
Scanning us. A kingdom in his brain,
this prince in threadbare jeans,
hard heels of his hiking boots flush
with the edge of a ravine that drops
from the path, a plunge so deep I cannot look.
A momentary loss of balance, gust of wind
would hurl him off the cliff into the Urubamba River.
I want to grab him by his cotton, white-sleeved shirt
and shout, Don't stand there on that edge!
I want to yank him to the middle of the path.
> See that black condor circling the pinnacle,
> spying on small prey? See those malevolent
> peaks the Spaniards scaled, lured by the gold
> face of a blazing sun?

3. Market at Pisac

Amazing how the sacred soil of the Uru-
bamba Valley nurtures this variety of spuds.
In the sprawled market in Pisac, piles of
white, russet, gold potatoes displayed
on blue plastic-covered tables or the ground.
Mangy dogs sniff avidly. The squatting
women planted, weeded, dug, lugged sackfuls
balanced on their broad backs up from the fertile
valley. Snaking through it on a bus you observed
the gossamer mist floating like morning ghosts
above the fields. When it lifted, the glorious,
golden sun shone through, spilling a benediction
on bowed heads, hats perched rakishly.
Children knelt as if in prayer. You waved at them
but they were busy begging the sacred earth
in which their small brown hands were buried
to release from her full breast (like gold)
the sweet abundance of potatoes.

4. Summit
(Altitude: 4335 meters)

How far above everything we are,
here on the Altiplano. Isolated.
Cold. Two gentlemen from Mexico
sit side by side on the tourist bus, upright,
jackets and manners beyond reproach,
their Spanish soft. Melodious.

Alpacas grazing on dung-coloured plains
look lonely too. Quechua women
have herded them since dawn
of time. A vertical roadside sign
proclaims in universal terms
our true position. Here

everyone's greedy for the meagre air.
We crowd around the shawled and shivering
women with sharp eyes, soft piles of merchandise.
We grab patterned hats, alpaca sweaters,
try them for size, slip into them.

Only the impeccable Mexican gentlemen
need nothing. At this dire elevation
they breathe in fluent rhythm, raise
with gold-ringed fingers their binoculars
and spy in silence.

Clouds stake out the ice-
blue territory up for grabs
above the summit of the distant, light-
tinged mountain ridge.

5. Elegy for a young girl

She is climbing her final mountain, agile
as the vicuna, dodging stones, shadows. The sun
haloes her head with gold. The honest wind
breathes unmistakably.

An entourage of men guides her ascent.
They don't intend to rape her, but no one doubts
she must die. (As I must,
trudging on, choosing easier trails each season,

breathing deep.) She knows
something is up. It's dangerous
to be chosen. To be born
with silk skin, eyes like ebony,

a puma's litheness. She is clever
enough to elude snakes, escape the condor,
for the chance, perhaps lucky
to be an Inca wife.

The men, merciful, brew coca tea.
The steep path shifts and twists, rocks teeter,
trees contort their dizzy arms.
She hardly feels the blow to her head.

Her body, lifelike, immaculate
and for a short time, warm,
abandoned to the puma and the condor.
The ailing Inca rises. Lucky.

At her age I had never seen a mountain.
My landscape, flat as an ironing board, was home
to prairie dog, jack rabbit, fox. The silent
osprey hovered overhead. I'd heard

how Jephthah's unnamed daughter, doomed
by a father's word, fled to mountains in Gilead.
Her teenaged friends, abandoning the timbrel, wailed
for a life cut short. The unborn children.

In Peru our guide said girls are honoured by such death.
He stopped speaking; I stopped, winded. Grief-stricken
like those unstained wailing girls I balanced against
such honour: amplitude of jade blue mountains,

radiant sun, wind hallowing our narrow trail.
I listened long and breathlessly,
like Jephthah,
for an echo.

6. Museum skulls

Each one deformed, deliberately.
These alterations are accomplished
when you bind a small head tightly
before the young bones harden. A child
chosen to receive an oddly elongated skull
is lucky. Is guaranteed more brain-
power, greater wisdom.

What mother wouldn't want these blessings
for her baby? In case of future complications,
headaches too fierce to bear, internal bleeding,
nausea, the tribal surgeon will be called to cut
a coin-sized circle in the skull, adult or adolescent.
An orifice through which the excess fluid flows.
Pressure is eased. Pain ceases.

Deftly, with a disc of hammered gold,
the diligent surgeon closes up the hole.
This large glass case adjacent to the skulls
contains the flattened metal rounds astonished
archaeologists removed from bones resting
in ancient graves. You may not touch,
but please observe them glittering.
                                Imagine
how Pizzaro's eyes would shine.
His round head spin.

7. At Saqsayhuaman

The taxi driver, his English fair to good,
says: Sexy woman, you wanna see
sexy woman? A mis-
pronunciation that's become
a come-on. Grinning,
he parks the taxi close as legal
to the ruined strumpet.

Open your hand, the guide says, place it flat
on the rock face. Trace with your fingers
clean lines between the rough-
shaped boulders hauled from a quarry
you can see from that steep ridge, a distance
of sixteen kilometres. A multi-sided
stone mates with five neighbours. Look how ardently
they fit. No one could slide a credit card between them,
or the sharpest blade. On the reverse side of the wall,
artisans—their skill worth gold—left gaps between
the rocks. Filled them with gravel and sand.
Cataclysmic tremors are absorbed when the aroused
Andes shudder and under you the whole earth moves.

The grinning driver waiting in his beat-up vehicle,
drinking coca tea, smoking, says:
Is that sexy or what?

8. Plaza de Armas

A Quechua woman, heavy-laden, shadows me
along the street, across the plaza, past the empanada
stand and up stone steps of the cathedral where a mother
arranges her costumed children, decorated animals
at various levels.

> Years ago in Klaipeda a German woman arrived
> with crèches she had collected traipsing around the world.
> Come Christmas, she would pack a hundred holy families up,
> schlepp them to post-Soviet cities. Joseph and Mary
> made of olive wood from the middle east, ebony from Africa.
> Jesus crafted from straw, felt, paper, carved from stone,
> swathed in burlap, linen, silk. The Magi's miniature caskets
> filled with smidgeons of incense, gold and myrrh.
> She showed me a plaster of Paris crèche she claimed
> Canadian Mohawk Indians made.

The tableau's ready for my camera: dolled-up children,
long-suffering llamas, alpacas innocent as lambs,
the cathedral's towering authority. Its cool shade.
I fumble in my bag for coins that shine like gold
but are not gold

and turn. The Quechua woman shadowing me
has laid out headbands, blankets she has made
from textiles woven by the village women.
Her clay birds whistle. Stones shine green and red.
Hammered bronze can replicate, amazingly, the sun.

She opens her brown hand to let me see
its calloused emptiness. Her smile is brave,
her skirt a flower garden in full bloom.

Email from Crimea

Tanya's flat had a room with a view: palm fronds
and chestnut leaves roofing the park. The greenery
encircled Lenin, his stony right hand raised, his eyes
fixed blindly on a snaking mountain trail, the summit
crowned with a crenellated fortress. The medieval
ruins overlooked the sea.

In the kitchen Tanya measured flour and oil.
Gas was disconnected years ago, the stove, like Ilyich
Lenin, left standing. A place for souvenirs
from Soviet times, keys to the flat, a favourite icon.
On a single electric element she cooked mountains
of *pelemenje* and *pilaf.*

Soviet years were better, Tanya said. She meant that
water flowed all day, not just one hour, cold, at dawn.
For the spirit it is better now, she mused, uncertain.
And the Black Sea always heals.
We removed our shoes and waded in, called out
for someone from the beach to take the picture.

There's Tanya, hand held high, defying the Crimean sun.
My tourist feet and hers lie buried in the sea. The stony
remnants of the fortress on the mountain rise,
prophetic. We raised our eyes and vowed
we'd climb up after supper. But the June sun dis-
regarded us as usual. It sank too soon.

This morning's email tells me Tanya had two strokes.
Knows no one, though her blue-grey, sightless eyes are wide.
She cannot speak of Soviet times, can't lift a hand
to hold a spoon, make *pelemenje*, greet the evening sun.
Her brain can't tell her feet to rise, climb hills.
I can not help
                but picture her a prisoner
in a room whose window frames a crumbling edifice,
abiding, palm-fringed statue,
and the Black Sea.

Wilderness Wandering

1. Drought

You think it's another weekend trek
into back country, knapsack crammed
with packets of edibles, bottles of potable
water? This is mirage country, the roaring
in your ears a gush that drives you crazy.
Crisis of thirst stays with you as you move
in slow stages from one dried-out gully
to the next. You are always waiting
for what the reluctant sky conceals,
approaching the end of hope. Scanning
the Lenten landscape for the rock that,
struck, spurts water.

2. Moriah

I had no idea, climbing, I was heading for a wilderness
experience. It began simply, an aging but still fit Dad
and his adolescent son setting out before the worst heat
beleaguered us. Mom had nervously packed snacks
and water. We carried equally the means of making fire.
Extra wood. Flint. A knife. As we ascended Mount Moriah
Dad muttered about relinquishment, nothing unusual. At mid-day
sun reached its zenith. The colour blue drained from the sky
and I felt oddly hollow hiking with this sweating, silent man.
Dad faltered off and on, disoriented. My feet felt weighted,
ground shifted underneath them. That day, begun like any other,
turned sinister, my father and I alien, that angel—wingspan
like the firmament, an upraised hand—was just another voice.
The knife a nightmare in our brains. We saw the wild-eyed ram,
its horns entangled in one of those curious thorn-bushes
that grace the wilderness.

3. Desert encounter

Desert at first glance is an absence
of vegetation. Imagine
Moses' astonishment, this blazing up of a shrub

he hadn't even noticed. Palace-raised,
he'd flamed as youths do for the underdog,
ready to finish off the nearest terrorist.

Beside this crackling bush he kicks his sandals off,
bewildered, argues till he's blue:
I'm not your man, my tongue is totally inadequate.

And (less theatrically, more honestly):
I'm really scared. In this vast wasteland
everything you know blurs,

shrivels in the heat. Cold swallows it
at night when any presence, any fire
is a welcome. Or a warning.

4. Simeon Stylites

If someone in jest had asked Saint Simeon, How's the view from the top
of a stone pillar? he would have faced them straight, surveyed his empty realm
spread like a sea around him. An errant wind, he might have said, sprang up
at noon, sent eddies whirling like a dervish, flung dust and grit into my face.
Decades of holding barnacle-tight to a firm position hones courage and conviction.
The sun has long burned off whatever is extraneous: abstraction, theory, flesh.
Stripped, Saint Simeon does not agitate for shade or shelter for the night.
No weight of heat, no silence has the power to shake him from the anchor.
The endless sand is visible from where he stands. A desert wind blows
where it chooses.

5. Found art

Pretend you are an aid worker in a helicopter
hovering over the remains of coastal villages.
An upturned ship several kilometres from shore,
sections of relocated railroad twisted like plastic
sticks, acres of collapsed cottages, palm trees
flattened like grass. Dung-coloured garbage.
Random installation without end. Spontaneous
patterns chaos makes from what existed.
A blast of air from the descending copter's
rotor picks up and shifts a piece of wreckage,
altering the original design. Picture
landing on ground where you discover
all you know is: nothing
that is living stirs.

6. Lines

Think of desert as the book of grief in which you write
everything that you have broken, that has broken you.
Use words like *bruised, stricken, betrayed,* engraving
sorrow on the page. Hold nothing back. Think of the wind
obliterating overnight the lengthy lines in sand.

7. The essential

desert is found near Carberry where flat prairie
surrenders inexplicably to hills, the land rising,
falling modestly. Keep going, going and before
you know it you have reached an ancient lakeshore.
Climbing white dunes along the laid-out, sun-
baked path exhausts the casual hiker. Finally
you reach the picnic table, unpack tuna sand-
wiches, apples, a thermos of tea. The brochure
names this bleak geography the Spirit Sands, a habitat
for wolf spider, pocket mouse and Bembix wasp.
When you have finished your tea, admired the way
shifting winds pattern and re-pattern the sand,
you may remember reading: every Jew, Gentile,
Muslim must sojourn like Abraham a good while
in the desert. Flab gives way to muscle, flesh to spirit,
when you inscribe footprints in the sand. Do not hesitate
and do not hurry.

The Stripped Garden

A bird sings, forceful, glorious as a pipe-organ,
And the huge bustling girth of the whole world
Turns in an everywhere of sunwardness
Among the cloudcarved sundering of its oceans.
—Margaret Avison

Thought Bird

The brown stirring you thought was a sparrow
harvesting grubs in high grass
is an oak leaf the north wind worried.
Last year's leaf. Dry but not decomposed.

A thought when it lights in the brain is a bird.
Can't stop it from landing on your head,
your mother said, but never let it build
tangled nests in your hair.

She meant messy thoughts, not those
that prompt visiting the poor, sick, imprisoned.
Not thoughts that render a house so spotless
there's not one scattered sock.

Once people believed this planet flat as a board.
A child running too fast, too far from centre
would arrive at the edge. Slide off. That edge,
these fine brains thought, was absolute.

Wouldn't you think a bird—starling, osprey, finch,
even an owl—could soar with impunity past any rim,
hover for a while above—what? Abyss? Apocalypse?
An utter abstinence? An idle thought.

While the bird flutters over emptiness,
proving it can be done, what
are the rest of us beset by?
Ennui? Excitement? Ecstasy? Or even

envy? Might give that some thought.
The brown leaf on the lawn is not dislodged.
The wind having let up, time having drifted on,
birds lighted, lifted off. At nightfall

it flutters still. As if alive. The mind,
shifting, has long lost interest.
Not one of the two-for-a-penny sparrows
will give it a second thought.

Episode

What had the flower to do with being white...?
—Robert Frost

Look how the feathers of the dying bird shine green.
Light lifts the indifferent afternoon. Beside the lane,
pruned branches, corn stalks, tangled tomato
vines bundled for the garbage.

You did not ask to witness the last twitch, the neck
trying to bend, delicate claws that will stiffen and splay.
Under the dun breast feathers a small heart
pumps its last blood.

You had not planned to ask what force lures accident
to a back yard. If there's foreknowledge
or intention when a creature after impact
with impassive glass or metal falls

consummately still. You are unwilling
to touch with ungloved fingers a thing
so recently alive, so newly dead, the feathers
sleek as if a cat's tongue licked them.

A mellow sun, traveling through the autumn afternoon,
sheds light on evening. On the dead bird.
(What steered the creature? Killed it? Who
knew the reluctant witness?) The loath grave maker

must kneel and bend to lift with warm hands
the lifeless body, lower it into a shallow
hollow in the stripped garden, and cover
with earth the soft, green-glowing wings.

Sanctuary at Ventes Ragas

Always our conversations wheel round to birds.
Light swims through the morning forest
we have entered, looking up

for the nest of a sea eagle. Empty,
it signifies: wrong season or the birds
murdered in a surge of blood lust.

At the sanctuary breasts of English robins
trapped in nets for banding pulse to bursting.
Flight vanquished. Lightness sabotaged.

In the village we are offered eggs, warm
from feathers of the brown hen.
Gaggles of querulous geese

gabble in worn grass. The equinoctial
afternoon blends French and English,
dialects of Lithuanian

interwoven with a bird-vernacular,
the wind wailing raw from the Baltic Sea.
We are speaking of the way birds weave

the same nest over and over, same old tricks,
faked broken wing, air-shattering
screech to drive intruders from their territory.

How is it in the village Kintai with its earthbound fowl
we debate functions of hooked beak and claw,
theories of flight, buoyancy?

We marvel how an eagle soars.
The falling of an English robin
brings it home to earth.

Genesis

Our mother planted her prairie garden in March,
covered the shriveled seeds with soil and watered them.
Before we knew it east windows burgeoned
with green pepper sprouts, parsley, tiny tomatoes.
We watched with ravenous hope. In March

my gardening friend turns her back to the blizzard
in the window, snowman grinning from the storm-
bound yard. She's curled on the couch, lost in glossy
Homes and Gardens, stuck between seductive pages
of seed catalogues. She's driving winter out with visions
of plump tulips, the first blue crocus breaking through.
Her fingers crave the warmth of summer earth.
Crave rain.

I'm skiing through a birdless wood, my head filled up
with gardens, gliding past aspen and oak, hawthorn
and barren birch, dreaming their empty branches green.
Dreaming this wintry world a tangle of lush vines, undergrowth
a person could get lost in. Orchids blooming pink and mauve.
The apple shining on a pristine tree. In its vicinity the serpent coils.
The carolling of newborn birds fills everything and everywhere
light (and the first thin shadow) shivers across the green.

Salvation

The garden across the fence tempts me.
Not the disconsolate phlox,
the cosmos' alarmed eyes eying me.
It's the apple tree I ogle, bold-as-brass
crabs bending the autumn branches, adornments
burdening the neighbours' tree. The old man's

heart is giving way. Can't raise his arms
above his chest, heft an over-filled basket,
clamber up the aluminium ladder.
He's lost all taste for apples anyway.
His wife can't tempt him with fresh *strudel,*
a flaky pie she's baked.

She too is losing heart. Losing desire
for picking, peeling, slicing. She hates
watching the apples fall, the lawn pocked
with fruit bruised beyond salvation. She pities
would-be plunderers, high-wire squirrels, the scarlet
evidence of thievery impaled on their teeth.

Help yourself, the old man says, fumbling
at the broken gate. His wife's gaunt body's
bent like a hairpin, rescuing crabs from grass.
She tries to straighten, waves me in-
to the stripped garden. Oblivious to a dozen
crows quibbling over portions of tart flesh,

she offers me a curious grin
and fills my hands with apples.

Flood

Let the floods clap their hands...(Psalm 98:8)

I have done it again, the river seems to say,
roiling northward, bearing ill-gotten cargo,
flotsam on a surface of gunmetal water.

All night in sleepless neighbourhoods the river
scales its banks, embraces ancient oaks,
rises to the lowest branches.

Uprooted tree trunks, thundering, collide
with bridge abutments.
Residents cry out, alarmed,

O River why have you betrayed us?

The river without ceremony breaks through concrete,
deposits evidence of industry, debris as calling cards
on couches. Carpets are water-logged.

Neither alarmed nor furious it churns triumphantly
north: to the lake. Only a fool would dare
step into a stream so stripped of mercy.

Above its quagmire banks, the huddled people
of the river listen to the torrent's unleashed
roar, and weep.

Lion

*We must build our arks with love
and ride out the storm with courage.*
—Frederich Buechner

The lion in a prairie zoo lies lazy
on his platform on a withered tree as if he's dead
or dreaming

a sudden motion in the grass. Black and white
stripes float like shadows in a warm brain
crazed with the tantalizing

smell of blood: that pair of zebras
within cubits of his claws. The water rising.
To kill forbidden on the ark.

Darkness of that cloud-veiled sky
above the rising water is like darkness
in the dozing lion-brain

or darkness of a prairie thunderstorm in summer
or like that afternoon the sun refused to shine:
God spread-eagled on a tree, the temple torn,

a cry as if a lion roared
and like the ghostly creeping in of dawn
the dead walking.

Vacation

Vultures at the garbage dump have commandeered
the limbs of a naked tree. Rows of attentive gulls
occupy a second skeleton. Their white feathers
and the vultures' black plumage alike attract the sun.

At the foot of the leafless trees a diligent rooting:
ten black bears chow down choice leavings
from lake cottages. Vacationing families pull up,
the glassed-in children counting birds and bears,

thanking their lucky stars.
'One smack of that black paw and your neck will crack,'
one tells the other. 'No one leaves the van,'
the parents warn their children.

The feeding bears disdain the sealed off audience.
The birds, prophetic on their segregated trees,
keep their feathered cool, their gloomy counsel,
and their black or white wings folded.

Kildonan Park

April and the muscle-shirted boys
park their hot cars, casually
fling out like errant Frisbees
their newly-deepened voices.

There's a catcher's mitt, baseball bat
and lots of balls but what the boys want
is girls perched on picnic tables
slathering sunscreen,

lighting cigarettes. Girls who will open
their pony tails to any wind that blows.
It whistles from the west, fresh
from ravaging the prairie. The boys

toss and catch and shout, *Hey, man.*
(Practising their baritone.)
Smoke floats like incense from the April girls.
Cool and without mercy,

they whip lipsticks out, crank up
the volume on boom boxes
and fling their brazen *njeah, njeah*
to the crows.

Occasion

Who will rescue me from this body of death?
Romans 7: 24

My mother began walking as if the wind
was always at her back, bending her forward.
Osteo the doctor said. A few excruciating
weeks and she lost inches, walked that way
a dozen years or more before she left us. She was thin.
Wind at her back would have swept her away.
One afternoon, doing her best to rise
to the occasion of my visit, she held her head up
high as she could and asked, astounded:
      Is this real
      or are we dreaming?
Did she mean the rocking chair, the bed, the open
window letting in the light? Me? Her bent self?
Her eyes though almost blind shone bright as planets.
Known boundaries blurred. She yearned to walk,
absolved, beside calm water, on cool grass.
Longed to sit upright, painless at the table,
able to lift with a steady hand the brimming
cup to her lips.

Eclipse

Our aunt broods at the curio cabinet, a stone in her chest.
Winter casts shadows on the boy caught in porcelain
lines of innocence. His fishing rod, his dog. She adores
the tip-toe dancer in a blue translucent skirt.
Sun brought dust to light this morning, cast sheen
on glass shelves, bestowed haloes. Winter's gift.
Fading, it left our aunt a portrait of sorrow,
every movement a lament. Not for love lost irretrievably,
a friend who's moved, a family member slipped away.
She touches with such unplanned melancholy the Lladro
figurine, carvings she bargained for in Italy, glass from Bavaria.
Evening light glanced from the Arno where she stood,
when she was young, halfway across the Ponte Vecchio.

The cabinet she bid for at an antique auction sale must go.
Our aunt must go into an EPH. A stripping down,
down-scaling. Stove and fridge, one window
facing north, a narrow bed. Knees, hips turned traitor,
heart erratic, ears unwilling to allow sound into the brain.
Tonight we'll coax our aunt onto the empty balcony.
Take these binoculars, we'll shout, and watch earth move
between the sun and moon. A shadow thrown over cold craters,
the remote Sea of Tranquility. Where you'd expect full darkness,
look, there's light: a canopy above the balcony. A rose glow.
The over-shadowed moon still visible. Venus bright.
The brittle stars unveiled.

Grace

Some days the body believes everything under the sun
has been wrung out of love. Clouds brought into being
and stacked like orange smoke over the staid horizon.
Over the city the moon. Shriek of a night train
cutting through sleep.
                    And the hand's particular shape,
rib cage curved to bunker the pumping heart,
knees fit for bending.
                    The body comprehends
scent rising like an invocation from the stove,
an offering someone's hand stirred. Our places laid;
cups filled to the brim. We wait for silence around the table
to be broken,
a voice that says *take, eat.*
and without fanfare, scarcely wavering:
Don't be afraid.

The night sky

Same old strangers (possibly astrologers,
possibly three) camel their usual way
from east to west crossing blank desert,
time zones. What they are heading for

remains unclear. Under the stingy sun
they trespass foreign fields, prod their animals
past lethargy. How quietly
the winter shadows lengthen,

landscapes shift as if creation, roused,
hopes for release. At nightfall they collapse
beside a meager waterhole. The (possibly hungry,
homesick) travelers before they close their eyes

look up. There is the moon, a flat white stone
embedded in ebony. The faithful constellations.
And just ahead that singular, unerring
blur of light to steer by.

Poems for Advent

There's a certain slant of light...
—Emily Dickinson

1.

He comes at last, the long-expected painter
in working clothes, carrying ladders, paint-
spattered dropsheets. He'll cover everything
and scan each wall for cracks
        caused by the building shifting,
plaster and scrape, making rough places plain.
If he's inclined he'll hum
        Lo how a rose ere blooming
while I remove from every room all hindrances:
the vining ivy, ornaments, those matched lamps
that might get in the way of things. Myself.

When everything is ready he'll begin.

2.

In church a small girl leans her shampooed
ribboned head against my arm and falls asleep.
I cannot rise to sing *O Come Emmanuel*
or kneel to pray.

Her breathing is a lullaby, her cheeks pink porcelain,
her chubby fingers splayed like stars.
Two candles flicker and the choir
sings: *Jesus Christ the Apple Tree.*

Three weeks before the incarnation and this child
dreams while the preacher's text from Genesis
probes the indifferent darkness that the light
appearing silently midwinter in a makeshift
cradle will overcome.

64

3.
I wanted to look up, just after sunset
for that rare conjunction of the planets
newspapers promised. Night after night
the southwest sky stayed dull, a sullen
overcast too thick to let light through. Now
the portentous pattern's gone, the evening
sky a blaze of constellations, lone planets,
dazzling lights of an aircraft coming home to land.

At Birds' Hill Park we ski by candlelight.
Someone's deployed at intervals along the trail
a hundred paper bakery bags half-filled
with snow, to hold lit candles. The flickering
dispels the darkness as we glide into and out
of modest radiance. At the warming hut
we sing, uncertain angels, our frail hope
for holiness and joy, munch Christmas cookies.

Reshouldering our backpacks, snapping
our skis back on, we move, warm shadows
through the silent night. The candles spent,
we scan the patient sky for shooting stars,
planes, planets, the remote progress
of an aging satellite.

4.
It's taken weeks to read this long
biography about a woman of whose life
little is known. Her poems are the map
from which the author reads the arduous
odyssey this Amherst woman undertook,
traces her ongoing quarrel with the Lord
God of Hosts. She fought with him as Jacob
at Peniel fought. For personal autonomy,
integrity. Fought for dominion. Blessing.
Only when the rest of Amherst almost
without noticing had laid to rest that
fervency of faith, when she had laid to rest
her mother, father, young friends who died
in childbirth, the incarnation gave her hope.
Good news passed on by word of mouth.
Rumour become credible at last. This tale
fills up the advent weeks, it keeps me waiting
as at Amherst, Emily, with obdurate resistance
waited for the light.

Rewinding Time

I still cannot shake off the superstition that the only past that is real, that exists at all, is the one contained within the memories of living people.
—Michael Ignatieff

Letters from Siberia

(Based on drawings and texts
by Jakob Sudermann, 1888-1940)

1.
Dear Gretel I am sending you
a butterfly a bee bunches of daisies
and a cat I had intended to send
a mouse also but it got away
not all mice are so quick
or so lucky

There are no butterflies here
no bees no daisies
it is winter and the ice thick
paper your mother sent
is gone the colours finished
when next I stumble upon
blank scraps the fortuitous
small stub of a pencil

I will draw the garden blooming
in my head and if they let me
I will send it I will leave it
to your mother to describe
fountains at Alexeyevka
carriage and matched horses
rose beds how the sun
warmed our world

she will tell you
I am the lost Onkel
whom you do not know
the one who sketched
a family dwelling painted
the orchard in autumn painted
your grandmother at prayer
or sewing painted the snow
that fell on the Dnieper River
and one day in spring
vanished

2.
Dear Gretel I can see my breath
all afternoon in the endless evening
stars are my candles how long
before a pinpoint of cold light
reaches me and keeps me
hoping the longed-for warmth is
somewhere on its way

don't be afraid if this should be
my last letter if the picture
of the garden I remember
never reaches you
the sun will rise rain fall
on Alexeyevka I believe
you will see spring

3.
Dear Gretel it is spring
your Onkel who is still as much
alive as the mangy cat
though aged imagines
himself in Alexeyevka
he is too weak to mount
the black stallion
climb the greening hills
too weak to imagine painting
the budding apricot trees
even the sun rising
earlier each day
can not warm him
after the long and bitter winter
a small grey mouse appeared
and this time it did not
escape

Slowly from the North
In memory of Sara Froese, 1924-2004

(A record of excursions
enjoyed or at least endured,
by a resident in a Personal Care Home.)

1. Cruise
At the railing of the river boat a woman
without strategy, sophistication, grace,
peers into the water. Sluggish. Opaque.
She wants to walk on it, indifferent
to prudent voices warning her: Don't go too far.

Far is where she's always been, too far
from centre, water, sun's warm light.
Wayward, she strays from home or shore,
a mapless wanderer whose feet itch
to leap like an antelope's over a rail.

She spits into the dark river,
observes the tiny whorl she's made.
How soon the slow boat leaves it far behind.
The sun slinks off. The river
cruise is over.

2. Interlude

There are geese at the lake's edge.
The curious woman walks toward them, bending
against the wind. Her breath erupts in short puffs,
her right foot drags. She calls out with a will:
I'm coming.
                      The wary geese,
oblivious to the import of her slow arrival,
stagger up from the water, rise honking to the sky.
Before she can say with confidence: *I'm here,*
they are gone.
                      Headed south.
Their sojourn on the water a small interlude.
The woman coming slowly from the north
stirred something in their blood.
She stares at the receding V, grieving.
Empty water, empty sky.
Arrival always from the wrong direction.
A sojourn just an interlude. Her steps
a stumbling at the water's edge.

3. Equestrian

At the stable bridled horses are led out for a trail ride.
The woman is reminded of her father's farm,
her brothers riding. (She was a child then, spirited,
always underfoot or over fences.)
                      She picks a dark horse
believing she can mount it, princess on a shining steed,
a queen reviewing troops, her whole kingdom.
Or better, a wild woman who loops her bold leg easily
over a stallion's bare back and clamping hot thighs
tight against the warm horse rides
whooping through the narrow gate.

4. Pleasure

Rain falls, a benediction on the modest garden,
but the woman wants the sun. She's dreaming
sweet hundreds bunched like small green grapes
have turned scarlet. She pops them in her mouth
one after another, bites them, splits the skin,
the juice runs where it will.

Hunkered beside the sprawling tomato bush,
hands, mouth filled, she forgets everything
is circumscribed, all pleasure measured out:
one modest helping of baked chicken, one
cookie made with sugar substitute, one
visit to the shopping mall per resident per season.

She wants the measuring stick thrown out.
Wants to wallow eyebrow-deep in pleasure
so magnanimous it flows, forbidden honey,
sweet and sticky down her chin.

5. Angle

From this angle the high rise building
presents its flattest aspect: complacent brick
measured in squares of glass,
the metal bars of balconies.

The angle is acute. The woman's got her feet
planted on pavement, neck bent
to decipher without squinting
the brazen: LEASING NOW.

Her head's exploding with imagined populations
trapped behind glass and brick. Steel bars
policing tiny rooms, each with its narrow bed,
one chair, cramped closet. On good days

a tall nurse steps on a stool, opens the transom
letting the outside in. Why shouldn't she
(the woman) be forgiven for imagining her life
repeated in those lofty, unknown rooms?

Why shouldn't high rise dwellers, after
hot tub, gin and tonic, be forgiven,
looking down, for overlooking
the woman on the pavement,

her firmly planted feet, impatient escort?
She holds her head at such a funny angle,
her neck must ache, the vicious summer sun
burning her eyes. Her brain spinning.

6. Departures

She remembers a teenager running from home
for the first time, possessions in a paper bag:
lemon-yellow sweater, a radio, her new shoes.
Doesn't know that she'll return or be returned.
That home's a place you leave
and think you've found and leave again.

The woman staring through the single window,
homeless, dreams escape. A flax-blue sky
flares wide as the scarf magicians conjure from a sleeve.
Sun skulks over frosted oak tree crowns,
skirting the day. Desired destinations
hemmed in. The restless woman

turns from the window, arrays herself
in a brand new thrift shop bargain coat,
a sky-blue scarf, scuffed walking shoes.
She fills plastic bags with underwear,
filched magazines, filched candy,
guts and gall.

Singing in her cracked voice *Halleluja,*
she will thrust her awkward body
at the wild north wind,
her mind like steel against the world,
against all doubt. She'll stumble forward
and again forward.

7. Story

Winter and the woman wants a story. The plot
uncomplicated, characters not too subtle,
not devious. No flashbacks to those harrowing
episodes best left behind. She wants the future
now, time a straight line. Wants bounties
poured out at her feet. Adventure.
And of course love.

                                Setting should be simple.
No rough ice-covered fields, this unforeseen
wind howling from the north.

She worries about the ending. Wants it thrilling
the way those screaming kids are thrilled
wooshing down the toboggan slide.
She wants to climb up with them, woosh down once,
just once before the end
she believes will take her breath away.
She wants the consummation sweet,
fantastic, daring
and dear Christ not too soon.

8. Wideness

One day the room she inhabits
will be stripped, scrubbed, carbolized.
In place of pictures, patches on the faded wall.

A three-car cavalcade will trace the rise and dip
of a ribbon road threading its slender passage
through the Pembina Hills. It will be summer

and the fields—Oh the wide fields!
Canola blooming yellow, flax periwinkle
blue. Sky cloudless until evening.

The cars will pass the corner where the family
farm stood. The green-roofed house. Garden and barns.
Wheat ripens at the intersection where she played, a child,

pulled in all directions. Her father used to say
(homesick for the sun-gold eastern steppes,
the nightingale at evening):

        Und die Stätte kennet sie nicht mehr.
        '...its place knows it no more.'

Remember (someone else will say) how straight and still
and like a child she lay in her narrow bed,
inhaled her last lungful of thin air, expelled it

with a gasp as if surprised
she wanted nothing, needed nothing more.
Feared nothing.

West winds will sweep the pine-crowned hill, the earth
open to receive her. Sky without a single cloud
and like an ocean, endless.

German Lessons in the Interlake

1. My mother taught me Gothic

Not early architecture, mansion with dark arches,
horse and a handsome rider, devious,
mysterious. Love on a haunted moor.

My diligent mother at the kitchen table
washed sticky porridge bowls while I
bent mesmerized to the plain brown book she'd sent for

from Germany. Father hewed oak and poplar down,
wrestled with sinister underbrush,
slapped querulous mosquitoes from his face.

Always beyond his reach, the golden grain fields,
fat cattle. Our mongrel, Rover,
collected woodticks, barked gophers away, crows,

the noisy wheels of vehicles. My tight-gripped pencil
practised slant lines. Sharp points of lower case,
looped flourishes of upper. Skin on my child knuckles

stretched taut and white as I repeated
at the kitchen table: *Mutter Vater Kind*
and also *Hund,*

while on our isolated road an alien wheel
snarling its fatal script
put full and final stop to Rover.

Tod,
my sombre mother taught me. A short,
uncomplicated word to end the lesson.

2. *Mittagschlaf*

After the noon meal a space opens
as if in the forest there's a clearing
where you least expected it, so crammed
with unbarred light you catch your breath.
Though no one ordered it, the wind that blew
all morning from the north keeps low
and in the grey lake past the silent trees
tranquil water holds a boat.

My father after *Mittag* orders me to wake him
when the long hand touching twelve
reaches three.

He shifts his aching limbs until they're settled,
sleeps fifteen minutes, dreams
he is floating in a sea of prairie wheat,
the acres free of obstinate oak roots,
unruly children, grasshoppers,
drought, mortgages, unwieldy stones.
Rain, sun, wind are measured out
in fair proportion.
                    In the grey lake
a weathered boat lies waiting.

3. Cherry orchard

August and the small clearing that surrounds
the weathered house is drowned in heat.
Hawks cruise the bleached sky silently.
White leghorns deep in dust baths.
In the shade of a hazel bush a mother
and her daughter shelling peas.

Daughter wants a winter blizzard
a cool wide lake, shade of that improbable
cherry orchard her mother's taken refuge in.
Kirschen the mother says.
Die Frucht so rot und rund.
Her hair and forehead dripping wet,
skirt stuck to her thighs.

                    The peas
freed by Daughter's sun-browned fingers
spring from the pod
while Mother's in another country
and Father in a heat-drenched field is making hay.
They leap like sea-green eager cherries
pip pip into the pail.

4. The violin

When darkness falls, Father
in his sweat-stained shirt, boots
caked with barnyard dirt
remembers the whirr and racket
of the factory, the foundry
in the distant village where the red hot
steel was hammered into ploughshares,
molten metal poured into a flywheel form.
Clank of steel on steel,
barked orders. He remembers
the way his blood sang.

It's Mother tells the children how he played
the violin and sang:

> *Hab oft im Kreise der Lieben*
> *im duftigen Grase geruht*
> *und mir ein Liedlein gesungen*
> *und Alles war wieder gut.*

The children make a circle in spring grass,
shape their small mouths to the melody. They imagine
Father's work-thick fingers nimble on the strings,
the sunburnt, leathery wrist bent gracefully
above the bow. Eyes closed,

he's in the secret place in that quaint melody
where all is well.

5. Gretel picking saskatoons

The Brothers Grimm got some things right:
a child lost in a forest must be someone's daughter
old enough to know you don't leave home
without a ball of string,
apron pocket full of white bread
crumbs to scatter. She knows better
than to give herself away by breathing hard.
Or running.

Thorny undergrowth baffles the father
who longs like a deer for water for cleared acres.
A hunter worth his salt would look to his gun,
look around. Wolves lurk in these thickets.
Even the wicked witch thinks twice before
she'll thrust another stick into the fire, hoping
something innocent will come her way.

Mother, heavy with the memory of winter,
leaves the house, calls her unwilling, half-grown
daughter to fetch a pail and *komm, komm schnell.*
They lift the barb wire strand and slip
with empty apron pockets into darkness.

Trapped in a stand of high-bush berries,
invisible wolves, echoes
of ringing axe-blows, the mother's urgency,
Daughter does not need anyone to tell her
the age-old story has begun
closing in.

6. Presence

In the blinding sky above the bush a vulture soars.
Omnipotent. Omniscient. Silent.
So high you have to bend your neck way back.
The grey wings fold. The predator
plummets
crashing through oak branches
straight for the dire, delectable
eyes of the red squirrel
cowering field mice
a garter snake.

Barefoot children quake at the austere presence:
God is in the interlake.
It's what mother means when she warns:
Kinder, ihr sollt lieb sein.

Anglo Saxon and Ukrainian
neighbours live untroubled by God's wingspan.
The terrible, swift arrival. The reason
neither children nor small animals
can wander after dark into the bush
with gladness and without
a wild heart beating.

7. Alphabet

Most likely the Winnipeg aunts
looted the Goodwill Store: tools, toys
for the children. It can't be the tiny
arthritic grandmother in her Mennonite shawl

wool-mittened in the middle of summer
and not one word of English.
She's not to blame for the twenty-six
blocks mailed to the interlake.

Apfel Affe Abendbrot.
Or *alt.* Like the grandfather
who clicks his weary glasses shut in Winnipeg
before he goes to bed.

Bett Brot Butter
Biene buzzing like crazy in July alfalfa fields.
Bäbi? The mother shakes her head and says
there can not be another.

One morning it is *Esel Ecke* and the next
grosz gelb gerade. The father walks *gerade*
from house to granary after his morning porridge,
buttered bread, two cups of *Prips* with milk.

By noon his intrepid shoulders slump.
At lunch he bows his head
and cannot see the children
mouthing 'apple' and 'ape'

'bread' and 'butter.' The bilingual
wooden blocks when Father isn't looking
whisper 'mittens' to the giggling children,
scream out 'more' and 'mine.'

But when Father lifts his head
opens his sobering eyes, his ears
hear nothing but the contrite chanting:
Mama Mimi Milch.

8. War in the interlake

The Winnipeg uncles on a summer Sunday
arrive in white shirts, white shoes.
They park their cars in a camouflage of poplars,
commandeer the living room and begin

arguing who will win: the Allies
who speak mainly English?
Hitler who is godless? The father
leaves to do the chores.

A fleet of aunts lands like butterflies
lightly in the bedroom. They park their babies
on the double bed and for a while
there's peace.

Behind the barn the oldest cousins have become
fighter pilots. Screened by the jadegreen
twisted branches of an oak they've occupied
the boys are winning.

The still-slim aunts before retreating
to the stifling dining room regroup
in mother's kitchen garden. Rows of entrenched
carrots. Cabbages assaulted by white butterflies.

Mother boils water for *ersatz* coffee.
A buzz of low German. A swift slaughter of flies.
Recipes, domestic news traded like prisoners.
Crossfire. Ceasefire. Truce.

The uncles' altercation escalates. It threatens
to boil over. They've moved from low to high
German to appease an uncle who has married in.
Father, back from chores, finds Hitler winning.

Appalled he tells his city brothers
all their sons, ambushed in the gnarled oak,
have abandoned pacifism, armed themselves,
identified the enemy

and every single mother's daughter
skirting a hostile hawthorn bush
is without compromise
returning fire.

9. Moon dreams

Evening all afternoon. A stiff and silver moon
waxes toward the winter solstice. Brittle sky,
lake with its frigid skin, barenaked trees,
the bedraggled sparrows shivering. Mother says:
Gut dass die Stube inside *ist*. She's quoting
a man she met who said it laughing. She
offers it to her restless children.

Steam from a boiling pot clouds mirrors, melts
black holes in every window.
Night closes in.
The imprisoned children want to break free
from the steam inside, from the bitter cold,
the boredom. Mother at her wits' end
says: *Jetzt aber schnell zu Bett.*

Under the covers her unruly children
while she frets or mends, dream
of bright-winged horses and a sleigh,
a hill where from the summit they lift off and fly
pell mell like summer sparrows to the moon.

10. The interlake angel

One Christmas I found a mechanical cat,
my brother a blue tin truck.
Not Santa Claus but Eaton's brought them.
Our father with bare hands drilled holes
in a poplar sapling, grafted in green branches
the English neighbours one farm north,
prosperous, pruned from their Yuletide spruce.
Our ingenious mother made a paper angel
while we slept. The thermometer's red tongue fell
to minus forty. In the morning:
diamonds in the kitchen wndow.

Und der Engel sprach.

> An angel tangled in the frozen aspen,
> her song a solid breath, her wings brittle,
> bare feet blue. A flock of shivering shepherds
> tending frost-coated sheep in snow. In the cold,
> cold barn, cold cattle munch their cud, each
> tail stiff as my metal cat's. Pressed resolutely down
> it sends the animal rattling across the drafty floor
> chasing a red ball. Brother's blue truck
> dodges burly donkeys, huge lethargic oxen, goats.
> Like my grey cat it stops shy
> at a manger where a stunned girl-mother
> listens to a newborn breathing in the straw.

Father as if he knew the wintry interlake
could use a blessing
read after morning chores
in his prophet-voice from Luther's gothic script:
Fürchtet euch nicht.

From the rigid aspen tree
while Mother poured fresh milk on porridge
rationed the sugar
the angel's partly thawed-out
Gloria reverberated.

11. Goethe in the Interlake

> *Über allen Gipfeln ist Ruh.*
> *In allen Wipfeln spürest du*
> *kaum einen Hauch,*
> *Die Vöglein schweigen im Walde.*
> *Warte nur, balde ruhst du auch.*
> —Johann Wolfgang Goethe

i.
Über allen Gipfeln ist Ruh.

The G is hard as the splendid rock top
of mountains in a picture book. The children know
landscape if it's real lies flat as Mother's cookie sheet,
moon sees everything. The fertile earth conceals
tenacious roots of birch, poplar father felled.
A lucky child finds pemmican
the buffalo hunters left.

Ruh means rest.
The R is rolled like the rumble of an avalanche,
stampeding buffalo.
No, softer. A tremor of the tongue.
After a day of roots and rocks,
Father, his sore back bent,
his breath a rumble in his windpipe,
sleeps at supper.

ii.
In allen Wipfeln spürest du
kaum einen Hauch.

Say the initial consonant in
Wipfeln like a V,
imagining the highest motion of birch trees
come to rest.
No wind.
No raucous V of autumn geese
beating their way through northern air
with strong wings. You can feel
nothing.

Hauch means breath. *Is* breath.
Breath ending with a faint catch.
Breezes that shivered the emerald
crowns of aspen, reeds, grass
are gone. Everything
held in. Your lungs
will burst.

iii.
Die Vöglein schweigen im Walde.

Say V like an F, W like V.

Daughter is walking along a path
Indian warriors carved through bush,
their lithe bows bent, their poisoned arrows ready.
Moccasined feet tread noiselessly. The daughter's

insanely pounding heart drowns out
the small cry of a sparrow.

Mother searching for stray cows
listens for clanging of the dull bell
hung from the leather strap around the neck
of the blue plodding cow.

She wants that pair of wicked crows to stop
their conversation.

iv.
Warte nur, balde ruhst du auch.

Father is first to find rest. He's buried
in a storm so pure it covers everything. At night
roofs and the moon crackle with frost.
Mother says he should have waited for the spring
when rivulets of melted snow run silver to the ditch.
When crocuses and yellow lady slippers bloom.

A stone grave marker offers consolation:
He is at rest.
At last.

Mother who for years was lost and couldn't find
her way home is next. Might have been the bush-
enclosed house she looked for, a place
she loved, hoping it would be there, waiting.
She is laid in the ground in spring,
trees greening.

And that leaves two: Daughter and her brother
in the autumn light, a moody sun
emerging from or hiding in the clouds.
Shrubs that in spring bloomed lose their leaves.

Daughter dreads dreams of Goethe's *Gretchen.*
Her brother fears *Erlkönig's* icy breath.

Not much to say or do.
There has to be at last
an end.
          Crow falling silent.
The blustery north wind
dying down.

Rewinding time

I leant upon a coppice gate
  When Frost was spectre-gray,
And Winter's dregs made desolate
  The weakening eye of day

   ....

The land's sharp features seem'd to be
  The Century's corpse outleant,
His crypt the cloudy canopy,
  The wind his death-lament.
      —"The Darkling Thrush," by Thomas Hardy

Above us the pewter clouds and in the graveyard
geese hunkering near the pond, wind-ruffled, their eyes stiff
with indifference. They honk at us once or twice and won't budge.
It is Hardy's landscape: *The Century's corpse outleant.*

      We have come to bury our father.
It could have been our brother, former colleague, a wife.

     A story silenced.
An era gone for good. We wade through gold and grief.
Wind tears at our hair, our sombre overcoats and over there
that green carpet spread to camouflage a mound of earth.
A machine removed it, making room for the abandoned body.
This one has a mouth organ wedged between its *rigor mortis* fingers.
Another may have held a rose, a favourite cuddly bear, a book
crammed with mystery or news. Or nothing.

      Over the closed casket
the preacher speaks in parables: wheat dropped into a black furrow
in spring.

      But it's late fall.
We've raked our lawns for the last time this millennium, reeled in
stiff plastic hoses, harvested carrots, covered our lily bulbs
with mulch, rose bushes with burlap, emptied the eaves. How quickly
it's come round again to this. Just yesterday we watched the elm trees greening,
the neighbour's kid in water past the limits of his brand new rubber boots.

Yesterday that pretty bridge spanning the pond had not been built, the city
had not sprawled north, the father in this coffin had not learned to breathe,
pick out a tune on his harmonica. Had not discovered speech, reading,
the tangled skeins of love.

Someone leans over the coffin, a gesture repetition makes familiar:
pulling apart the fern, gerbera daises bright as the sun, lilies like cold snow.
You turn and walk away dismayed: how briefly anything that's beautiful,
that you most love, can last. Whole centuries of moments, days
scattered like petals.

                    Goose droppings dot the yellow grass,
the flat bronze markers bearing beloved names. When we are gone
the machine will come, the last gold maple leaves will fall, snow
that before the cars speed off could cover everything.

                         We will all,
some of us only once, some often, soon, come here again.

Coffee and fancy sandwiches. Uncommon leisure for retelling
a father's life. Those unfilled gaps in the beginning of the story.
A different country, an abandoned boy. If not for love
extended unexpectedly.... Isn't love always a surprise?
Home a hymn, a benediction?

                    There was music in his blood
and planted in his brain hunger to fashion something new
from something old, hold in his restless agile hands
hammer and saw.

                    A ship crosses the ocean.
We push aside our cups, imagine a curl of smoke. An insignificant
dot on the horizon coming closer to the future
until the travellers at the railing spy the *land's sharp features.*
Gulls plummet and circle as we reel off alien names,
letting them slip familiar from our lips: Halifax harbour. Montreal.
Beechy, Saskatchewan. Niverville, Manitoba.
Clearbrook and Winnipeg.

Years of labour.
We say it and sigh while the grandkids brag:
Opa built Santa's village. It's true: he made displays for Eatons,
may have whistled while he worked, measured a tune, nailed
anger down, carved out a resolution to endure the course.
Fitting that the day he died the whole department store shut down.
And all the miniature cultivators, John Deere tractors, plows he made
from scraps with his retired hands. Used all of his allotted
three score years and ten and lived past eighty.

A minor player
in this almost spent millennium. Outshone by centuries of stars glittering
upon the stage, the playing field, the battle field, the information highway.
His structures and his songs eclipsed by new-found laws of relativity
and probability, quantum physics, mystery of DNA.
New planets added in his lifetime.

We become silent.
Now it's *the weakening eye of day*. Night closing in.
The millennium's *corpse outleant*.
A father buried.

The future imminent,
who'd want to chronicle ten centuries of floods, the lethal shifting
of tectonic plates, shocking tsunami. Year after year drought's devastation.
Wars, rumours of war, continents gorged on plague, genocide and waste.
And always some fanatic with his finger on the trigger.

But each *Brief History of Time* that sets down an expanding,
savage universe, has also this: springtime and harvest, snow and rain
and that warm stirring in the earth. A rainbow after supper
in the east. Comets we stayed awake to gape at, curious or terrified,
in every century, in heat or frost.

Remember
how we lay at midnight on the dock our father built, dizzy
watching the summer meteor showers? Radiance
that streaked across the utter dark reflected in the lake.
Satellites in silent progress through the solar system.
Our faces heavenward, stars in our eyes, we all believed
that we were falling,
falling into sky.

And always wind and sun contending
without end as if all living were a fable.

Which story and what star guided us?
Was there a *darkling thrush* warbling *some blessed Hope*
we scarcely heard or were completely unaware of?

Like Lear we stumble, blind and foolish, through the wilderness
mourning our wayward children. Or straddle tragedy like Ben
Heppner singing Tristan on TV. The tenor rising like a newborn star
before Isolde dies.

Before he died, our father
told us, by heart, stories of another country. Spoke of going home.
He didn't mean the wind-whipped shack in Beechy,
farm house in Niverville, the white suburban bungalow in Winnipeg.
And not that unexpected home across the ocean. Nor was this planet,
in his mind, his only home.

The pewter clouds have opened up a slit to let light through:
blood dappling the sullen sky. The coffee's cold. In future as in past
the wind blows where it chooses. We also must go home.
We are waiting for the snow, another camouflage. For music to ring out
the old, summon the new. As if our father's hand had once again
raised the harmonica, his warm lips breathed a new song into it.

Notes

The composer of "African *Sanctus*" is David Fanshawe
The quotation in "The Weight of Opulence" is from Revelation 12:1
Ventes Ragas is located on the Baltic Sea
EPH: Elderly Person's Housing
The quotation in "Wideness" is from Psalm 103:16

Translations for "German Lessons in the Interlake":
  Mutter, Vater, Kind, Hund, Tod (mother, father, child, dog, death)
  Mittasgschlaf (afternoon nap) *Mittag* (midday or the noon meal)
  Kirschen, die Frucht so rot und rund. (Cherries, the fruit so round and red.)

The German verse in "The violin" can be translated:
  Often, encircled by loved ones,
  Resting in fragrant grass,
  I'd sing to myself a melody
  And all was well at last.

  komm schnell (come quickly)
  Gut das die Stube inside ist (Good thing, that a room is inside)
  Kinder, ihr sollt lieb sein (Children, be good)
  Apfel, Affe, Abendbrot, alt (apple, monkey, supper, old)
  Bett, Brot, Butter, Biene, Bäbi (bed, bread, butter, bee, baby)
  Esel, Ecke, gross, gelb, gerade (donkey, corner, large, yellow, straight)
  Prips (a coffee substitute)
  Jetzt aber schnell zu Bett (Now quickly to bed)
  Und der Engel sprach (And the angel said) *Fürchtet euch nicht* (Don't be afraid)

The lines by Goethe can be translated:
  All the mountain peaks are at rest.
  In the tree tops you perceive scarcely a breath.
  The forest birds keep silence.
  Wait patiently, and soon
  you too will be at rest.

Acknowledgements

I am indebted to Catherine Hunter for her generous help in preparing the manuscript, and to the editors of the following publications in which some of these poems have previously appeared: *Arc, Canadian Literature, CV2, The Fiddlehead, The New Quarterly, The Malahat Review, Other Voices, Spirit Mourn, Spirit Dance* (United Church Publishing House). The poem "Rewinding Time," first titled "Retrospective," received the National Magazine Gold Award for 2000.

"Ballad" by Denise Levertov is from *Levertov: Collected Earlier Poems 1940-1960* (New Directions, 1979).

"Easter" by Margaret Avison is from *Always Now*, Vol.1, by Margaret Avison (Porcupine's Quill, 2003).

"The World is not Conclusion" and "There's a certain slant of light" by Emily Dickinson and "Design" by Robert Frost are found in *Literature: An Introduction to Reading and Writing*, ed. Edgar V. Roberts (Prentice Hall, 1998).

The quotation from Michael Ignatieff is from *The Russian Album* by Michael Ignatieff (Penguin Books, 1979).

Most of the paintings referred to in the first section are included in *The Gaze of Love: Meditations on Art and Spiritual Transformation* by Sister Wendy Beckett (HarperSanFranciso, 1993).

Details about Emily Dickinson's life are taken from *Emily Dickinson* by Cynthia Griffin Wolff (Knopf, 1986).

The Saddest Music in the World is the title of a 2003 Guy Maddin film.

Previous Books by Sarah Klassen:

The Peony Season (2000)
Simone Weil: Songs of Hunger and Love (1999)
Dangerous Elements (1998)
Violence and Mercy (1993)
Borderwatch (1991)
Journey to Yalta (1988)